1 MONTH OF FREE READING

at

www.ForgottenBooks.com

By purchasing this book you are eligible for one month membership to ForgottenBooks.com, giving you unlimited access to our entire collection of over 1,000,000 titles via our web site and mobile apps.

To claim your free month visit:
www.forgottenbooks.com/free25424

*Offer is valid for 45 days from date of purchase. Terms and conditions apply.

ISBN 978-0-265-35895-5
PIBN 10025424

This book is a reproduction of an important historical work. Forgotten Books uses state-of-the-art technology to digitally reconstruct the work, preserving the original format whilst repairing imperfections present in the aged copy. In rare cases, an imperfection in the original, such as a blemish or missing page, may be replicated in our edition. We do, however, repair the vast majority of imperfections successfully; any imperfections that remain are intentionally left to preserve the state of such historical works.

Forgotten Books is a registered trademark of FB &c Ltd.
Copyright © 2018 FB &c Ltd.
FB &c Ltd, Dalton House, 60 Windsor Avenue, London, SW19 2RR.
Company number 08720141. Registered in England and Wales.

For support please visit www.forgottenbooks.com

STATUE

OF

JOHN BRIDGE,

THE

PURITAN.

SEPTEMBER 20, 1882.

CAMBRIDGE:
TRIBUNE PUBLISHING COMPANY.
1883.

City of Cambridge.

ACCEPTANCE AND UNVEILING

OF THE STATUE OF

JOHN BRIDGE, THE PURITAN,

PRESENTED TO THE

CITY OF CAMBRIDGE, SEPT. 20, 1882,

BY

SAMUEL JAMES BRIDGE.

STATUE ERECTED ON CAMBRIDGE COMMON, AND UNVEILED
NOVEMBER 28, 1882.

CAMBRIDGE:
TRIBUNE PUBLISHING COMPANY.
1883.

STATUE OF JOHN BRIDGE, THE PURITAN.

INTRODUCTORY.

IN the "Genealogical Register," which forms the supplement to Paige's "History of Cambridge," is the following: —

"BRIDGE, JOHN was among the earliest inhab. of Camb. and owned land here in 1632. He resided in 1635 at the N. E. corner of Dunster and South Streets, and soon afterwards owned a house at the N. W. corner of Holyoke and Winthrop Streets. About 1638 he purchased a house near the spot where the Washington Head Quarters now stand, with twelve acres of land, and resided there. He was early elected Deacon of the church; was Selectman twelve years, between 1635 and 1652; Representative four years, from 1637 to 1641; and was frequently employed in the settlement of estates and in determining the boundaries of towns. He m. Elizabeth Saunders 1658, (marriage contract dated 29, Nov. 1658,) who had previously been the wife of Roger Bancroft of Camb. and Martin Saunders of Braintree. He d. about 1665, leaving wife, son Matthew and granddaughter Dorcas, dau. of S. Thomas, deceased. His wife Elizabeth subsequently m. Edward Taylor of Boston and was living in 1685."

The subject of the foregoing notice had one son, Matthew, who survived his father, dying April 28, 1700, when upwards of 80 years old. The remains of father and son were deposited in the burial-ground in Harvard Square. Memorial stones were placed over their graves and over that of a descendant, Levi Bridge (hereinafter mentioned as the founder of the Bridge Charitable Fund in this city), July 4, 1876, by Samuel J. Bridge, the donor of the statue of the first of the name.

Shortly after the city of Cambridge was the recipient of a donation from another member of the family, the late Mr. Levi Bridge, who, by a deed of trust, dated Aug. 12, 1875, gave the sum of $773.95, which had been deposited in the Cambridgeport Savings Bank in the name of the late Hon. John Sargent as trustee. It was stipulated in the deed that, after the death of

Mr. Bridge, this sum was to be transferred to the city of Cambridge, and a statement of the facts relating to the gift was made by the trustee in a communication to the City Council, dated Sept. 6, 1876, the donor having deceased.

By the provisions of the deed of trust, the money thus given was to form the nucleus of a fund to be known as the "Bridge Charitable Fund," to be forever held by the city upon this further trust, to add the interest of said fund to the principal, until such time as said fund, by the accruing interest, or by gifts from other philanthropic persons, shall amount to two thousand dollars, after which time one third part of the interest of said fund shall be added to the principal annually forever, and the remaining two thirds of such interest shall be paid over annually to the overseers of the poor for the time being, to be by them expended for the deserving poor of the city of Cambridge, in such manner as they shall deem best."

The donation of Mr. Bridge was formally accepted by the City Council, Sept. 27, 1876, and an ordinance was subsequently adopted creating a board of commissioners of the fund thus established. The bank-book was delivered to the commissioners by Mr. Sargent, Jan. 24, 1877, the sum on deposit then amounting to $891.83. In the month of October following, this sum was doubled by the gift of Mr. Samuel J. Bridge, who was a distant relative of the original donor, thus making the total amount given to the fund $1,783.66. In the letter from Mr. S. J. Bridge, dated Oct. 15, 1877, covering the gift made by him, he said, referring to the original donation by his kinsman: "It was his wish, and it is mine, that beyond a proper record, there may be no unnecessary publicity in the annual distribution of the fund, nothing that would have a tendency to wound the pride of the recipient." In this communication, allusion is made to the graves of his ancestors, John and Matthew Bridge, and of his kinsman Levi, over which he had caused the erection of memorial stones, and the hope is expressed that the city "will always have a fostering care over them."

Samuel James Bridge, who will hereafter be especially remembered in this community as the generous donor to the city of Cambridge of the statue of the first of his name in this country, is a native of the State of Maine, where many of the descendants of John Bridge still reside. He removed to Boston many years ago, and in the year 1841 was appointed by President Harrison as an appraiser in the Boston Custom House, where he remained until 1856, when he was appointed appraiser-general of the Pacific Coast. His unwavering fidelity to the trust reposed in him by the Treasury Department while appraiser for the port of Boston, is well remembered by the older merchants of that city. Mr. Bridge had the confidence of every administration of the national government from the time of his appointment in 1841 to the close of the administration of President Grant. He was the commissioner having charge of the erection of the Custom House at San Francisco, costing $5,000,000; and also of the United States Mint and Marine Hospital in the same city. In his later years he has travelled much, visiting every quarter of the globe, and by his rare powers of observation has made himself familiar with the characteristics, institutions, and population of nearly every country in the world.

The commission to execute a bronze statue of John Bridge, the Puritan, was given by Mr. S. J. Bridge to the eminent sculptor, the late Thomas R. Gould, of Boston, in the autumn of 1881. He designed and modelled a statuette, which was satisfactory to Mr. Bridge, and subsequently carried it with him to Florence, where he arrived on the first of November. Preparations for the clay model of the "Puritan" were soon after begun, and about the 23d of November the artist personally worked upon the statue for the first and last time, also giving suggestions in regard to certain changes desired. Mr. Gould died on the 26th of November, 1881, and the completion of the figure devolved upon his son and co-worker, Marshall S. Gould, who devoted his entire time and energy to the execution of his father's conception of the "Puritan." In advancing and completing the work, he made such changes from the small model as had been previously suggested to him by his father, together with such alterations as every artist finds necessary in making a colossal statue from a diminutive study. The names of T. R. and M. S. Gould are thus properly connected in the production of the finished work,— the one as the original designer of the statue, the other as the skilled and appreciative co-worker, than whom none could have more fully realized the father's conception of the character to be produced in monumental bronze.

It has been said that this generous and artistic gift is believed to be the first statue of a Puritan pioneer that has been erected in New England. Through the pious forethought of the donor, it is also the first sculptured representation of one of its early settlers that has been set up in the city of Cambridge.

The stormy periods of our early history have heretofore been commemorated by us from time to time, and such localities as have been rendered historical through their association with leading men and events of the past have been marked by memorial tablets placed at different points in our city. To Samuel James Bridge, now for the second time the city's benefactor, must be accorded the merit of having brought to our view the lineaments and figure of the Puritan himself, as idealized in the artist's mind.

CITY OF CAMBRIDGE.

Statue of John Bridge, the Puritan.

AT a meeting of the Mayor and Aldermen, Sept. 20, 1882, a communication was presented by his Honor the Mayor, from Samuel James Bridge, Esq., of Boston, offering to the city a bronze statue of his ancestor John Bridge, one of the first settlers of the town, and an active and useful man.

The kind offer thus made was met with an appreciative spirit by the City Council, as appears by the following order, which was adopted in concurrence: —

CITY OF CAMBRIDGE,
IN BOARD OF ALDERMEN, Sept. 20, 1882.

Ordered, That the statue offered to the city by Samuel James Bridge be accepted, and that the thanks of the City Council be given to Mr. Bridge for his generous offer.

Also that a joint special committee, to consist of his Honor the Mayor, and Aldermen Read, Corcoran, and Fairbanks, with such as the Common Council may join, be appointed to take such action as may be proper in relation to the reception of the statue and the selection of a location for the same.

Sent down for concurrence.

Attest: JUSTIN A. JACOBS, *City Clerk*.

IN COMMON COUNCIL, Sept. 20, 1882.

Concurred. The President, with Councilmen Bent, Pear, Russell, Doyle, and Thorogood, are joined on the part of this board.

Attest: J. WARREN COTTON, *Clerk*.

Approved, Sept. 21, 1882.

JAMES A. FOX, *Mayor*.

The Joint Special Committee thus appointed was composed as follows: —

>His Honor JAMES A. FOX, *Mayor*.
>Alderman JOHN READ.
>Alderman MICHAEL CORCORAN.
>Alderman JOHN W. FAIRBANKS.
>President GEORGE H. HOWARD.
>Councilman GEORGE C. BENT.
>Councilman ISAAC S. PEAR.
>Councilman WILLIAM E. RUSSELL.
>Councilman JAMES E. DOYLE.
>Councilman JOHN G. THOROGOOD.

The commitee immediately proceeded to the duty assigned to it, receiving assistance in the suggestions of William S. Barbour, Esq., city engineer, and Marshall S. Gould, Esq., the sculptor. After visiting several localities in the vicinity of the former abode of John Bridge, the committee finally selected a spot deemed suitable as a site for the statue upon Cambridge Common. There was a slight delay, owing to the non-arrival of the statue from France, where it was cast, and on account of the illness of the donor, with whom the committee wished to consult in reference to the location to be selected, and whose views it was desired to meet in the fullest manner.

The general superintendence of the work of locating the statue was committed to Mr. Barbour, city engineer; the labor of putting in the necessary foundation, placing the pedestal thereon, and setting up the statue, being performed by Mr. Alexander McDonald, of this city. The granite base was firmly set, and the statue placed in position under the immediate supervision of the sculptor, and the work was completed on Saturday, Nov. 25th, after which it was covered to await the inauguration ceremonies. The statue is located in that part of Cambridge Common, near the junction of North Avenue and Waterhouse Street, and faces in a nearly southerly direction, looking towards the College grounds. The figure is about nine feet in height, and that of the pedestal about the same, the entire structure being about eighteen feet from the foundation.

The day of the formal acceptance and unveiling of the "Puritan" was fixed for Tuesday, Nov. 28th, at 3 o'clock, P. M. It was intended by the committee that the ceremonies should take place around the base of the statue, but a fall of snow and subsequent cold weather intervening, it was decided to ask that Shepard Memorial Church, on Garden Street, opposite the Common, be opened for the purpose. The attention of the public had been called to the occasion, through the various local newspapers, all being invited, while special invitations were also sent to a large number of prominent citizens and others. A special form of invitation was also sent by the donor to the descendants of John Bridge, numbering as far as known one hundred and thirteen in all, including one infant seven months old, of the ninth generation from his ancestor.

CITY OF CAMBRIDGE.

This city invites you to be present at Cambridge Common, on Tuesday, November 28th, at 3 P. M., at the ceremonies attending the acceptance of a statue of

JOHN BRIDGE,

one of the founders of the town, presented to the city by Samuel James Bridge, a descendant in the sixth generation.

For the Committee of Arrangements,

JAMES A. FOX, MAYOR.

Cambridge, Nov. 20, 1882.

CITY OF CAMBRIDGE.

This city invites the descendants of John Bridge, one of its founders, to be present at Cambridge Common, on Tuesday, Nov. 28th, at 3 P. M., at the ceremonies attending the acceptance of a statue of their ancestor, presented to the city by

SAMUEL JAMES BRIDGE,

a descendant in the sixth generation.

For the Committee of Arrangements,

JAMES A. FOX, MAYOR.

Cambridge, Mass., Nov. 20, 1882.

The invitations to descendants of John Bridge were sent to the following: —

NAMES.	RESIDENCES.
Samuel James Bridge	*San Francisco, Cal.*
Mr. and Mrs. Nathan William Bridge	*West Medford, Mass.*
Jane P. Bridge	*Somerville, Mass.*
Edmund Bridge	*West Medford, Mass.*
Frederick William Bridge	*West Medford, Mass.*
Mr. and Mrs. James Bridge	*Augusta, Me.*
Susan Williams Bridge	*Augusta, Me.*
Margaret North Bridge	*Augusta, Me.*
Sarah Cony Bridge	*Augusta, Me.*
Ruel Williams Bridge	*Augusta, Me.*
James Bridge, Jr.	*Atlanta, Ga.*
Horatio Bridge	*New York City.*
Joseph Hartwell Bridge	*Leadville, Colorado.*
Hannah North Bridge	*Geneva, N. Y.*
Anna Frazier Bridge	*Geneva, N. Y.*
Mr. and Mrs. William Bridge	*West Medford, Mass.*
Henry Saunders Bridge	*West Medford, Mass.*
Edward W. Bridge	*West Medford, Mass.*
Helen W. Ritchie	*Philadelphia, Pa.*
Lucy Perkins Bridge	*West Medford, Mass.*
Eliza Putnam Stone	*Boston, Mass.*
Mary Bridge Vose	*Colorado.*
Hannah North Vose	*Colorado.*
Chandler Vose	*Colorado.*
George Howe Vose	*California.*

NAMES.	RESIDENCES.
Hannah Bridge Williams	Augusta, Me.
Abby Williams Marble	New York City.
Horatio Bridge	Washington, D. C.
Charlotte Marshall Bridge	Washington, D. C.
Margaret North	New York City.
Hannah E. North	New York City.
George Weston	New York City.
Mary Austin	New York City.
William F. Bridge	Foster's Crossings, Ohio.
James Crosby Bridge	Foster's Crossings, Ohio.
Elizabeth Crosby Bridge	Exeter, N. H.
Henry Whitney Bridge	Cincinnati, Ohio.
William F. Bridge, Jr.	Cincinnati, Ohio.
Herbert Sage Bridge	Cincinnati, Ohio.
Catherine May Bridge	Foster's Crossings, Ohio.
Walter Guild Bridge	Foster's Crossings, Ohio.
Josiah Bridge	Cambridge, Mass.
Mrs. William T. Piper	Cambridge, Mass.
Charles Bridge	Albany, N. Y.
Charles Francis Bridge	Albany, N. Y.
Erastus T. Bridge	Haverhill, Mass.
Mrs. Samuel Bridge	Cambridge, Mass.
Mr. and Mrs. George O. Davis	Lexington, Mass.
Frederic Gardner Davis	Lexington, Mass.
Charles Bridge Davis	Lexington, Mass.
Harry Wellington Davis	Lexington, Mass.
Alice C. Baker	Cambridge, Mass.
Mr. and Mrs. George L. Stratton	Concord, N. H.
Florence Gardner Stratton	Concord, N. H.
George Bridge Stratton	Concord, N. H.
Charles Devens	Boston, Mass.
Thomas M. Devens	Charlestown, Mass.
Martha Lithgow Downes	Charlestown, Mass.
Caroline Devens Morris	Portsmouth, N. H.
Henry Devens	Brattleboro, Vt.
Francis Payson Sherburn	Charlestown, Mass.
Edward F. Devens	Charlestown, Mass.
Helen Devens Crocker	Charlestown, Mass.
Richard Devens	Washington, D. C.
Mrs. Arthur L. Devens	Cambridge, Mass.
Mary Devens	Cambridge, Mass.
Arthur Lithgow Devens	Cambridge, Mass.
Agnes Devens	Cambridge, Mass.
Frank Payson	New York City.
Charles Payson	Washington, D. C.
Francis Faithful	Brighton, England.
James N. Bowman	Council Bluffs, Iowa.

NAMES.	RESIDENCES.
Lizzie Y. Bowman	Wiscasset, Me.
M. W. Bridge	Providence, R. I.
W. W. Bridge	Wilbraham, Mass.
M. Wells Bridge	Springfield, Mass.
Benjamin B. Bridge	East Brookfield, Mass.
Jesse F. Bridge	Meriden, Conn.
Charles A. Bridge	Boston, Mass.
C. S. Bridge	Boston, Mass.
Mrs. Sarah Knowles Gibson	Boston, Mass.
Caroline Knowles	Boston, Mass.
Mrs. Rebecca Bridge	Boston, Mass.
Mrs. Abel E. Bridge	Waltham, Mass.
Theodore E. Bridge	Boston, Mass.
Mrs. C. T. Jackson	Concord, Mass.
Mr. and Mrs. Frederick Dodge	Concord, Mass.
Mr. and Mrs. William Arthur Mayor, U. S. A.	Governor's Island, N. Y.
John Jackson	Boston, Mass.
Lillie Jackson	Concord, Mass.
Charles Jackson	Concord, Mass.
Mrs. Stephen Barrett, Jr.	Ayer Junction, Mass.
Mathew Bridge	San Francisco, Cal.
William D. Bridge	New Haven, Conn.
Mrs. William Barber	San Rafael, Cal.
Wm. H. Bridge	Marblehead, Mass.
Robert Bridge	Marblehead, Mass
Edward Bridge	Marblehead, Mass.
Mrs. Isabella Freeman	Sandwich, Mass.
Bowman B. Johnson	Dresden, Me.
Elizabeth W. Gerry	East Lexington, Mass.
Charles Downing	Newburg, N. Y.
Henry Garfield	Cleveland, Ohio.
William Garfield	Cleveland, Ohio.
Mr. and Mrs. James McDonald	Boston, Mass.
John H. Sherburne	Boston, Mass.
Charles Morris	U. S. Army.
Caroline L. Hoy	Washington, D. C.
Gertrude M. Burnham	Lowell, Mass.
Caroline Watson	Charlestown, Mass.
John W. Bridge	Lawrence, Mass.
John W. Bridge, Jr.	Lawrence Mass.
Benjamin Hartwell Bridge	Lawrence, Mass.

[Seven months old, in the ninth generation from John Bridge.]

Unveiling of the Statue.

The services connected with the unveiling of the statue of the "Puritan" on Cambridge Common were held, in accordance with previous arrangement, in Shepard Memorial Church, the members of the city government, invited guests, and citizens generally assembling informally at the hour appointed.

The church was well filled, among the audience there being many distinguished citizens, conspicuous among whom was the venerable donor. There were also numerous other descendants of John Bridge, including Nathan William Bridge, Esq., of West Medford, Mass., and Judge Charles Devens, of the Supreme Court of Massachusetts.

Services.

The opening exercise was the performance of a voluntary on the organ by Edwin L. Gurney, organist of Broadway (Cambridge) Baptist Church, at the conclusion of which Alderman John Read, chairman of the committee of arrangements, made the following announcement: —

FELLOW CITIZENS AND GUESTS: — We are assembled at this time for the acceptance of the statue of John Bridge, the Puritan. I invite the Rev. Dr. Alexander McKenzie to invoke the divine blessing.

Rev. Alexander McKenzie, D. D., of the Shepard Memorial Church, then offered prayer, at the conclusion of which the audience joined in singing the following hymn, accompanied by the organ: —

HYMN BY REV. LEONARD BACON, D. D.

O God, beneath thy guiding hand,
  Our exiled fathers crossed the sea;
And when they trod the wintry strand,
  With prayer and psalm they worshipped thee.

Thou heard'st well pleased the song, the prayer:
  Thy blessing came; and still its power
Shall onward through all ages bear
  The memory of that holy hour.

Laws, freedom, truth, and faith in God
  Came with those exiles o'er the waves;
And where their pilgrim feet have trod,
  The God they trusted guards their graves.

And here thy name, O God of love,
  Their children's children shall adore,
Till these eternal hills remove,
  And spring adorns the earth no more.

Alderman Read: —

"The statue which will be unveiled immediately after these exercises is the work of the late Thomas R. Gould, completed by his son. It is of one who, having held offices of high trust, was a representative man of the early times. Samuel J. Bridge, a descendant in the sixth generation, has made this gift to the city of Cambridge, and his letter of presentation will now be read by George H. Howard Esq., the President of the Common Council."

President George H. Howard then read the following letter:

BOSTON, Sept. 20, 1882.

To the Honorable JAMES A. FOX,
    Mayor of Cambridge:

Sir, — I beg to offer to the city of Cambridge, through you, a bronze statue of my ancestor, John Bridge, one of the first settlers in the town, and a man useful and influential in his day and generation.

The sculptor, the late Mr. T. R. Gould, has tried to figure forth the Puritan pioneer, and upon the pedestal for the statue I have caused to be described the typical services and character which seem to me to make John Bridge worthy of lasting commemoration.

If the City Council accepts this offer, I shall ask leave to set up the statue in one of the public squares of Old Cambridge, the exact site to be determined in whatever way may seem to the Council suitable.

I have the honor to be, Sir, with respect,
    Your obedient servant,
        SAMUEL JAMES BRIDGE.

Mayor Fox accepted the statue in behalf of the city as follows: —

FELLOW CITIZENS: — From the communication of Mr. Samuel James Bridge, dated Sept. 20th last, to which you have just listened, you are informed that that gentleman — not now for the first time, I may say, a liberal donor to us, and happily present with us to-day — has presented this statue of his sturdy and heroic ancestor to the city of Cambridge, — believed to be the first statue in Puritan garb that has been erected in New England.

With becoming acknowledgment, the generous and artistic gift was promptly accepted by our City Council, and now being set up on our principal public ground not far from the spot of his early home on Dunster Street, we have assembled together formally to accept the finished work.

It gives me great pleasure to be the recipient, in behalf of the corporation and the citizens at large of Cambridge, of this statue of one of the early Puritans and settlers of our ancient and favored town from one his worthy descendants in the sixth generation.

John Bridge must indeed have been "a man useful and influential in his day and generation." Born in 1578 in old Braintree, in Essex County, England, during the reign of Queen Elizabeth of brilliant fame, he came in 1631, at the mature age of fifty-three, and settled here, as the inscription upon the pedestal states. He was our original supervisor of the public school, first townsman or selectman for twenty-three years, representative to the Great and General Court for four years, and was appointed by that body to lay out lands in this town and beyond.

We find his name prominently mentioned in the early records of the town in connection with those of Dunster, Hooker, Shepard, and others.

"Among the reasons," says the Rev. Thomas Shepard, "which swayed me to come to New England, divers people in Old England of my dear friends desired me to come here to live together, and some went before and writ to me of finding a place, one of which was John Bridge."

But I will not go into detail on these points, and thus encroach upon the province of the accomplished gentlemen who are to follow me, and who will illustrate the lives and the times of our Puritan progenitors much more ably than I can do.

It is surely well to "remember the days of old," and the men as well, who, by their sacrifices in any department of human endeavor or toil, have set forward the state of human progress on earth; and it is particularly fitting to erect statues to perpetuate the forms, the character, and the labors of our Puritan ancestors, that coming generations as they rise may not forget those devoted pioneers of freedom in religious truth and observances who preferred to emigrate to an unknown and inhospitable land, where they might worship God according to the dictates of their own consciences, rather than to wage a long and doubtful conflict with the strongly entrenched ecclesiastical system of England, united as it was to the complete civil power of the kingdom.

The Puritans brought to this land the highest principles of religious and civil liberty; and if we would witness the ultimate outcome of their principles, we may well say, with the epitaph in St. Paul's Cathedral, London, on the great architect of that church, "Look around you."

This statue has been executed by an American artist of genius and exquisite taste, of whom we have good reason to be proud, the late Thomas R. Gould, a native of Boston, but who long dwelt and wrought in Florence, Italy. His untimely death left the unfinished work to his son, Mr. Marshall S. Gould, who has admirably and successfully completed the original design of his father. The elder artist has impressed his genius upon many portrait statues and busts in this city and vicinity. In yonder library of Harvard University is his fine bust of Ralph Waldo Emerson; the Town Hall of Lexington contains a statue of John Hancock; while in the Public Library Building of Concord is one of its liberal donor to the town, William Munroe. By commission from the Grand Army of the Republic, he executed the beautiful statue of the noble Andrew which stands in the burial lot of our great war governor at Hingham-by-the-Sea. New York City claims a bust of the elder Booth; while in the vestibule of the Boston Herald Building his artistic illustration of steam and electricity may be admired. His portrait statue of King Kamehameha the First, at Honolulu, is a notable one, as well as that ideal conception entitled the "Ascending Spirit," which is appropriately placed on the burial lot in Forest Hill Cemetery where the mortal remains of the talented sculptor now repose.

And now need I repeat, as the representative of the city, that I accept with pride and pleasure this statue of the devoted Puritan and non-conformist, so liberally and handsomely bestowed by Mr. Bridge? and we will ever preserve it amid its pleasant surroundings with especial care, so that it may teach to our children's children to a late generation the courage, the self-denial, the humble yet heroic religious spirit of as brave and honest a body of Christian adventurers as, acting under their own light, have ever existed, who did so much towards setting forward the Redeemer's kingdom upon earth, and who so honestly labored to establish on this western continent what they deemed to be a great good, viz., "A Church without a Bishop, and a State without a King."

After the close of his address, the Mayor said : —

"A descendant of the Puritans has been invited to speak to you to-day. I take pleasure in introducing Col. Thomas W. Higginson."

Col. Higginson then delivered the dedicatory address of the occasion, as follows : —

The man whose name we to-day commemorate represents none of those classes which have hitherto almost monopolized bronze and marble. He was neither general nor statesman, neither poet nor author. No encyclopædia records his name, no history of the nation mentions him. Is it not strange that under these circumstances we should meet to dedicate his statue? On the contrary, it is for this very reason. It is a characteristic of the rising art of America, that, unlike the art of older nations, it celebrates the common man. Yonder silent figure upon our soldiers' monument does not wear the uniform of the brilliant general of cavalry, whose name heads the inscription below, but that of the hundreds of private soldiers whose names follow. It is the same with nearly all of the thousand other soldiers' monuments throughout the land. In the same way, going back to the Revolution, we have French's "Minute-Man" at Concord. Following the same instinctive tendency, going back to the settlement of the country, we have before us not Winthrop, not Endicott, but the private soldier, or at most the non-commissioned officer of the early Cambridge settlement, the typical Puritan, plain John Bridge.

It is the first time, so far as I know, that the every-day Puritan has appeared in sculpture. In the time when the clergy were kings or viceroys, this man was content to be a deacon. In the time when this very Cambridge Common, where we stand, was the scene where governors were elected, John [Bridge was satisfied with an office which is to this day a school of humility, and was member of the " Great and General Court." He was, in the expressive phrase of that day, a "townsman." He stands for the plain people, who founded the little settlement, and built for their defence the great " pallysadoe " and " fosse " which once passed within a rod or two of where the statue stands, and which have left their memorials to this day in the willow-trees of yonder play-ground. John Bridge probably worked in person on those defences; he was one of those who kept back the Indian and brought civilization forward; he stands for the average ancestry of us all. Whatever we now possess we owe, in a general sense, to the fact that our forefathers were even such men as John Bridge.

But, beyond this, we owe a peculiar debt to him individually. It happened to him to be instrumental, in a special way, for preserving the very existence of the little settlement. He came to America in 1631, probably as a member of a company from Braintree, England, which settled first near Mount Wollaston, and then was removed hither by order of the General Court, being soon joined by Rev. Thomas Hooker, who became their pastor. John Bridge came to Cambridge, then Newtown, in 1632; owned land here in that year, and became a freeman March 4, 1635. He lived at that time on the northeast corner of Dunster and South Streets, owning also a house on Holyoke Street soon after. In 1636 came an event which very nearly brought about the extinction of the little settlement. Parson Hooker, moved by the earliest outbreak of what has since been called the Western fever, made up his mind that the village, with its sixty-two houses, was too crowded for him and too near other villages. This was at least the nominal reason why he and the bulk of his congregation resolved to set off through the woods to Connecticut with wife and child, bag and baggage, cows and oxen, there to establish a transplanted Newtown at what is now Hartford. It is very possible that this formidable secession might have been the death of the little town, but for one fact, that John Bridge decided, in his sturdy Puritan spirit, to stay where he was and save the settlement.

The way in which he saved it was this: There was at that time in England a young clergyman named Shepard, not yet thirty years old, but of such repute for piety and eloquence that he has come down to posterity with four resounding epithets forever linked to his name, — " the holy, heavenly, sweet-affecting, and soul-ravishing Mr. Shepard." We know from his own autobiography that he came to America by the urgent request of friends; but the only friend whose name he mentions is John Bridge. He came at the most opportune time, with a company of sixty, and was persuaded to remain temporarily, at least, in Cambridge. He and his party stayed permanently; they took the meeting-house of Mr. Hooker, the dwelling-houses of his parishioners; and when, upon a day in June in 1636, Mr. Hooker and his hundred men, women, and children went with their oxen and cows through the streets into the wilderness, Mr. Shepard and his sixty stood at their newly acquired front-doors and bade them farewell. Exit Hooker; enter Shepard: but John Bridge was the link between. He was like the French herald whose duty it was to proclaim the king's death and the accession of his successor. "*Le roi est mort, vive le roi.*" It would have been strange indeed if when the new church was organized John Bridge had not become its first deacon. He was, as the facetious Cotton Mather would undoubtedly have said, had he but thought of it, " the *Bridge* that carried us over."

And, as it turned out, by securing Mr. Shepard he secured not the town only but the college. That was placed here partly for the sake of the climate, but more for Mr. Shepard's sake. It was because of him, Cotton Mather tells us, that this, " rather than any other place, was pitched upon to be the site of that happy seminary." There was thus a regular chain of circumstances. It was because of Deacon Bridge that Mr. Shepard came; because of Mr. Shepard that the college came; because of the college that the name came, taken from the English university town. Whether John Bridge was or was not identical with the "Mr. Bridges" who gave the infant college £50 in 1638, and who united with others in giving it £20 worth of goods four years after, this cannot now be determined; but the point beyond question is, that he indirectly secured its presence in Cambridge and all the advantages that have come to both college and city from the combination.

Under such circumstances, John Bridge began the duties of what an English poet calls the "mild diaconate"—not so mild then as now. In those days, when the village and parish were one, the minister was commander and the deacon was orderly sergeant. In that capacity John Bridge may have personally beaten the drum which was used in 1636, according to Johnson, to call the people of the village to church. At any rate he doubtless superintended the offices of the church, and the schooling of the children, so far as it went; he was deacon for twenty-two years, selectman for twelve years, and member of the Legislature for four. He was frequently employed in the settlement of estates and in determining the boundaries of towns. He was one of the commissioners appointed by the town when Billerica was set off from it, and his son was one of the first settlers of Lexington, both of these towns having been included in the unwieldy Cambridge of that day. John Bridge's own homestead was outside the village, and included twelve acres not far from where Craigie House now stands; he also owned a strip opposite, on the south side of the Watertown road, and running to the river. It included five acres of marsh and one of upland, perhaps including part of the very field across which our poet Longfellow loved to look at the winding Charles. In this homestead, then a rural region, he lived until his death in 1665; and it is pleasant to find that his son, in transferring a part of the real estate at a later period, describes it as "the mansion house of my honored father, deseased." It is not always that sons remember to express respect for their fathers when disposing of their property.

It is in a similar feeling of respect to that worthy man that we honor his monument to-day. Bronze corrodes and marble crumbles, but they are, nevertheless, among the most permanent of earthly things; and this modest

Puritan name will take long life from this event. One of the most famous of modern English sonnets describes an imaginary traveller in the East as finding in the desert two vast and trunkless legs of stone, with a carved and broken head resting near them. On the pedestal appears, —

> "My name is Ozymandias, king of kings,
> Look on my works, ye mighty, and despair."

And the poet adds: —

> "Nothing beside remains. Round the decay
> Of that colossal wreck, boundless and bare,
> The lone and level sands stretch far away."

But of what consequence was this desolation? The statue fulfilled its object. The disappearance of all else only vindicated the foresight of the monarch, and the name of Ozymandias is immortal. And thus the pious reverence of the descendants of this plain Puritan will achieve its end. The name of John Bridge, rescued from oblivion and made the type of the founders of our civilization, is destined to be transmitted on the lips of children's children yet unborn.

When Col. Higginson had concluded, the Mayor said: —

"From what has been said by the orator of the day, there is no doubt that John Bridge, whom we commemorate, was deeply interested in education, and might have been a worker in its behalf in the early days of our college. It seems eminently fitting, therefore, that a representative of that college should be heard upon this occasion. I introduce to you President Eliot."

President Eliot said: —

"What is this durable monument in stone and bronze to say to us and to coming generations? It will say, —

"It is good to stand stoutly in one's lot, doing faithfully and generously the homely duties of each day.

"It is good to leave behind sturdy and thrifty descendants to transmit one's name and recall one's memory through long generations.

"It is good to have one's life, though humble and obscure, represent to posterity great ideas.

"The simple life of this Puritan pioneer in barren Newtown foretold the life of the teeming millions who in two centuries were to vivify the wild continent. It was a worthy vehicle of three pregnant principles, — freedom of thought, political freedom, and freedom to worship God."

Mayor Fox: —

"You have heard from a descendant of the Puritans, you have also heard from the representative of Harvard College; let me now introduce to you a lineal descendant of John Bridge himself, General, and now Judge Devens."

Judge Devens' Address.

Mr. Mayor: — As a descendant from John Bridge, one degree further removed than my kinsman whose graceful liberality has presented this statue of our ancestor to the city of Cambridge, I thank you for the opportunity of being present upon this occasion. There is little to remind us in this splendid city, adorned with the buildings of its great university, in external things at least, of the humble hamlet defended by its palisade in which a band of exiles struggling with the stern soil, the inhospitable climate, the hostile savage, sought to make for themselves a home in which they could worship God according to the dictates of their own conscience.

It may be true, it no doubt is true, that there are others equally worthy to be commemorated with John Bridge, yet as he has been described to us in the remarks of Col. Higginson, to whose researches we are all sincerely indebted, as its first townsman for many years, as the deacon of its church, as its representative in the councils of the infant colony, he is a suitable representative of the founders of this town. He is in this place also a suitable representative of that great race of men to whom he belonged, the English Puritans.

The Puritan emigration to New England was a part of the struggle which had already commenced between King Charles and his people. However that might end, one place they were determined should exist where they should be free to practise their own faith and to act as that taught them. Profound as was their belief in a higher power, they knew that God works by human means and agencies, and that it was for them to endeavor to compass that for which they prayed by all the instrumentalities at their command. They believed in the sword of the Lord and of Gideon, but the sword of Gideon for them was the good weapon that hung in their own belts, and whose hilt was within the grasp of their own strong right hands.

We may imagine, if we cannot know, the intense interest with which, during the years John Bridge lived here, these people watched the progress of that English Revolution which has made of all who speak the English tongue a free people. Here they heard of the open war in England between their king and his Parliament, of the first doubtful and undecided conflicts under the inefficient commanders on behalf of the Parliament, of the rise of the great Puritan soldier Cromwell, of the victories of Naseby, Dunbar, and finally of Worcester, and of the complete triumph of the Puritan party. Here, too, came later the sad news of that September day when the Lord Protector sank to his eternal rest, and the way was open for the return of the king to England. Although he heard of all these events, John Bridge did not live long enough to know of the second English Revolution which was so promptly responded to in Massachusetts and which finally drove the Stuart kings into exile. To him it may have seemed as if this contest had failed. He certainly could not have realized how vast was the work which the Puritans had done and were to do on this as well as the other side of the water, or how great was the impression they would make on the people of a vast continent.

Mr. G. W. Curtis has said, " Through all our history, from the deposition of Andros to Bunker Hill, and from the Declaration of Independence to the Proclamation of Emancipation, the dominant power in American civilization has been the genius of Puritan England."

If we look back to the days of the Revolution we see how strong was its influence over those who conducted it. Mr. Winthrop, who (I may, without impropriety say, now that he is absent from us and separated by the stormy sea) emulates so well the dignified and scholarly virtues of his illustrious ancestor, has in one of his recent orations preserved a letter of Col. Prescott which might in its spirit have been written by one of the Puritans themselves. I quote it from memory, and not with entire verbal accuracy. " Our forefathers," says he, " passed the vast Atlantic, spent their blood and treasure that they might enjoy their liberties both civil and religious, and transmit them to their posterity." . . . . " Is not a glorious death in defence of our liberties better than a short and infamous life, and our memory to be had in detestation to the latest posterity? Let us all be of one mind, and stand fast in the liberties wherewith Christ has made us free: and may he of his infinite mercy grant us deliverance out of all our troubles! "

This was a letter written on behalf of the farmers of Pepperell to the inhabitants of Boston some months before the battle of Bunker Hill. As we stand here we recall that summer night of the 16th of June, 1775, when the two regiments selected by Prescott, one his own, the other commanded by Col. Ebenezer Bridge of Lexington, the great-grandson of John, stood here upon this very Common together, and the venerable president of the College came from his study to invoke the blessing of God on their expedition.

Nor, Mr. Mayor, when the hour of trial came in our day and generation to us, was the influence of these Puritan forefathers absent. It is at such a time they will always be freshly remembered. Let then this statue stand, in its simple Puritan garb, in memory of one of the founders of this city, of the race of men to whom he belonged, and in honor to their simple lives, their high courage, and their unswerving faith.

At the conclusion of Judge Devens' address, the audience again joined in singing a hymn with the organ accompaniment.

HYMN. — "AMERICA." J. S. DWIGHT.

God bless our native land!
Firm may she ever stand,
 Through storm and night;
When the wild tempests rave,
Ruler of wind and wave,
Do thou our country save
 By thy great might.

> For her our prayer shall rise
> To God above the skies,
>   On him we wait;
> Thou who art ever nigh,
> Guarding with watchful eye,
> To thee aloud we cry,
>   God save the state!

A benediction was then pronounced by Rev. Edward H. Hall, of the First Parish Church, and the audience then adjourned to the Common to witness the ceremony of unveiling.

The Unveiling.

When all had reassembled around the statue, which was entirely covered with cloth, Mayor Fox spoke as follows: —

" This statue of John Bridge, the Puritan, presented to the city of Cambridge by one of his descendants in the sixth generation, having been formally accepted, it is my direction that it be now unveiled."

At the signal of the Mayor, the folds of the covering quickly separated, and it fell to the base of the statue, disclosing an undoubted impersonation of the typical Puritan, in whose stern and resolute countenance is fully reflected the strong character of the men who founded our New England institutions of freedom and education.

The following inscriptions are upon the pedestal of the statue:

[FRONT.]

JOHN BRIDGE

1578-1665

LEFT BRAINTREE, ESSEX COUNTY, ENGLAND, 1631
AS A MEMBER OF REV. MR. HOOKER'S COMPANY
SETTLED HERE 1632
AND STAID WHEN THAT COMPANY
REMOVED TO THE CONNECTICUT.
HE HAD SUPERVISION OF THE FIRST PUBLIC SCHOOL
ESTABLISHED IN CAMBRIDGE 1635
WAS SELECTMAN 1635-1652
DEACON OF THE CHURCH 1636-1658
REPRESENTATIVE TO THE GREAT AND GENERAL COURT 1637-1641
AND WAS APPOINTED BY THAT BODY TO LAY OUT LANDS
IN THIS TOWN AND BEYOND

[BACK.]

ERECTED
AND GIVEN TO THE CITY
SEPT. 20, 1882,
BY
SAMUEL JAMES BRIDGE,
OF THE SIXTH GENERATION
FROM JOHN BRIDGE.

[RIGHT.]

THEY THAT WAIT UPON THE LORD
SHALL RENEW THEIR STRENGTH.

[LEFT.]

THIS PURITAN
HELPED TO ESTABLISH HERE
CHURCH, SCHOOL
AND REPRESENTATIVE GOVERNMENT
AND THUS TO PLANT
A CHRISTIAN COMMONWEALTH.

Lightning Source UK Ltd.
Milton Keynes UK
UKHW011004061118
331795UK00007B/106/P